TOWNS AND CITIES

By Claire Llewellyn
Illustrated by Anthony Lewis

RIGBY
INTERACTIVE
LIBRARY

Contents

City Life 4

Looking for a Job 6

From Villages to Towns 8

Lots of Homes 10

Getting Around 12

Under the Streets 14

This edition © 1997 Rigby Education
Published by Rigby Interactive Library,
an imprint of Rigby Education,
a division of Reed Elsevier, Inc.
500 Coventry Lane
Crystal Lake, IL 14

Text copyright © Claire Llewellyn 1996
Illustrations © Anthony Lewis 1996

All rights reserved. No part of this publication may be reproduced or transmitted in any form or by any means, electronic or mechanical, including photocopying, recording, taping, or any information storage and retrieval system, without permission in writing from the publisher.

Printed and bound in Italy
00 99 98 97 96
10 9 8 7 6 5 4 3 2 1

Library of Congress Cataloging-in-Publication Data
Llewellyn, Claire
    Towns and cities / by Claire Llewellyn ; illustrated by Anthony Lewis
        p. cm.
    Includes index.
    Summary: Introduces facts about cities and towns, such as the jobs available in cities, how towns developed, where people live, and how recreational time is spent in cities.
    ISBN 1-57572-197-X (lib. bdg.)
    1. Cities and towns--Juvenile literature. [1. Cities and towns. 2. City and town life.] I. Lewis, Anthony, 1966- ill. II. Title
HT119.L59 1997
307.76--dc21   96-52728

Old and New 16

Fresh Air? 18

Green in the City 20

Free Time 22

Index 24

City Life

A city hums, like a hive full of bees. Trains rattle, the traffic roars and planes drone high overhead. In the streets there are thousands of busy people, walking fast, always in a hurry. How did they all come to live in the city?

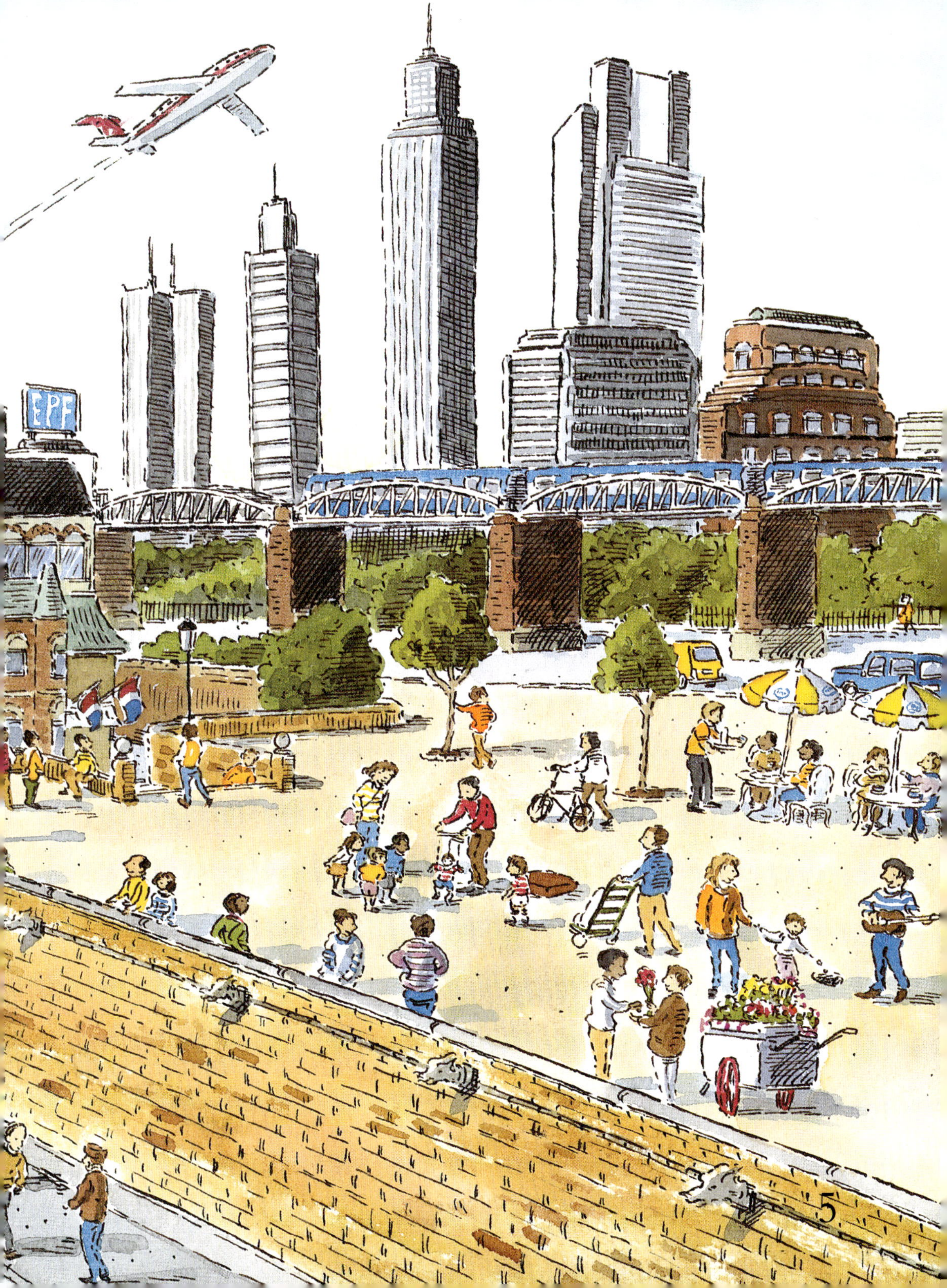
EPF

Looking for a Job

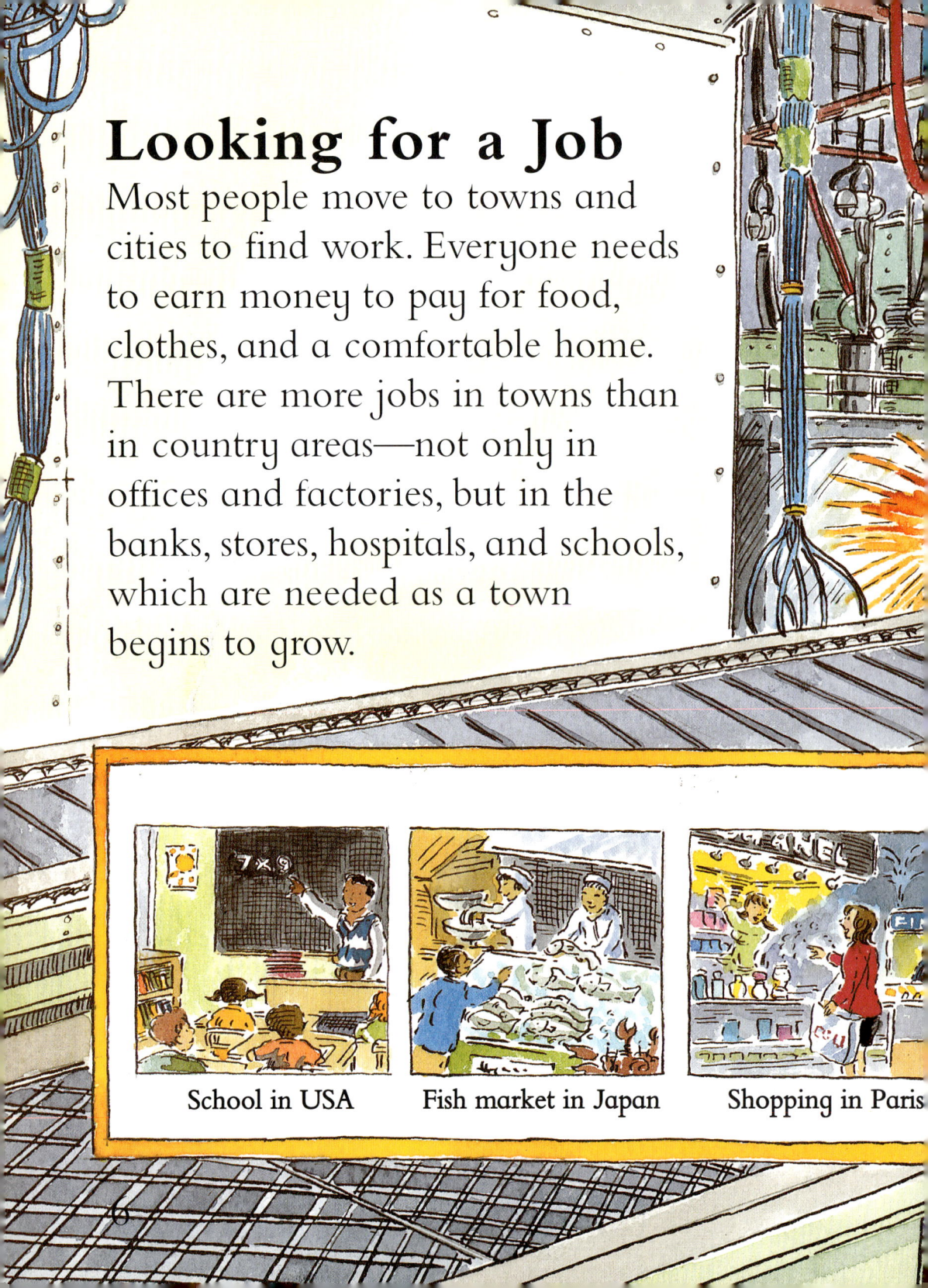

Most people move to towns and cities to find work. Everyone needs to earn money to pay for food, clothes, and a comfortable home. There are more jobs in towns than in country areas—not only in offices and factories, but in the banks, stores, hospitals, and schools, which are needed as a town begins to grow.

School in USA   Fish market in Japan   Shopping in Paris

Banking in Germany | Hospital in Sweden | TV factory in Singapore

From Villages to Towns

Most big towns were villages once. Year by year, they grew a little bigger—some, because they were on a river, and could send products up and downstream. Others, perhaps, became popular because they were by the sea and attracted visitors.

A seaside resort

As people lived longer and the population grew, more and more houses were built on the land, and the village became a town.

Lots of Homes

Thousands of people live in towns and cities. They all need homes to go to at night. Many of them live on the edge of the town, where the houses have yards and the streets are quiet. Others live in apartments in the city itself. Apartment buildings use less land, but there's nowhere to play.

Playing in the yard

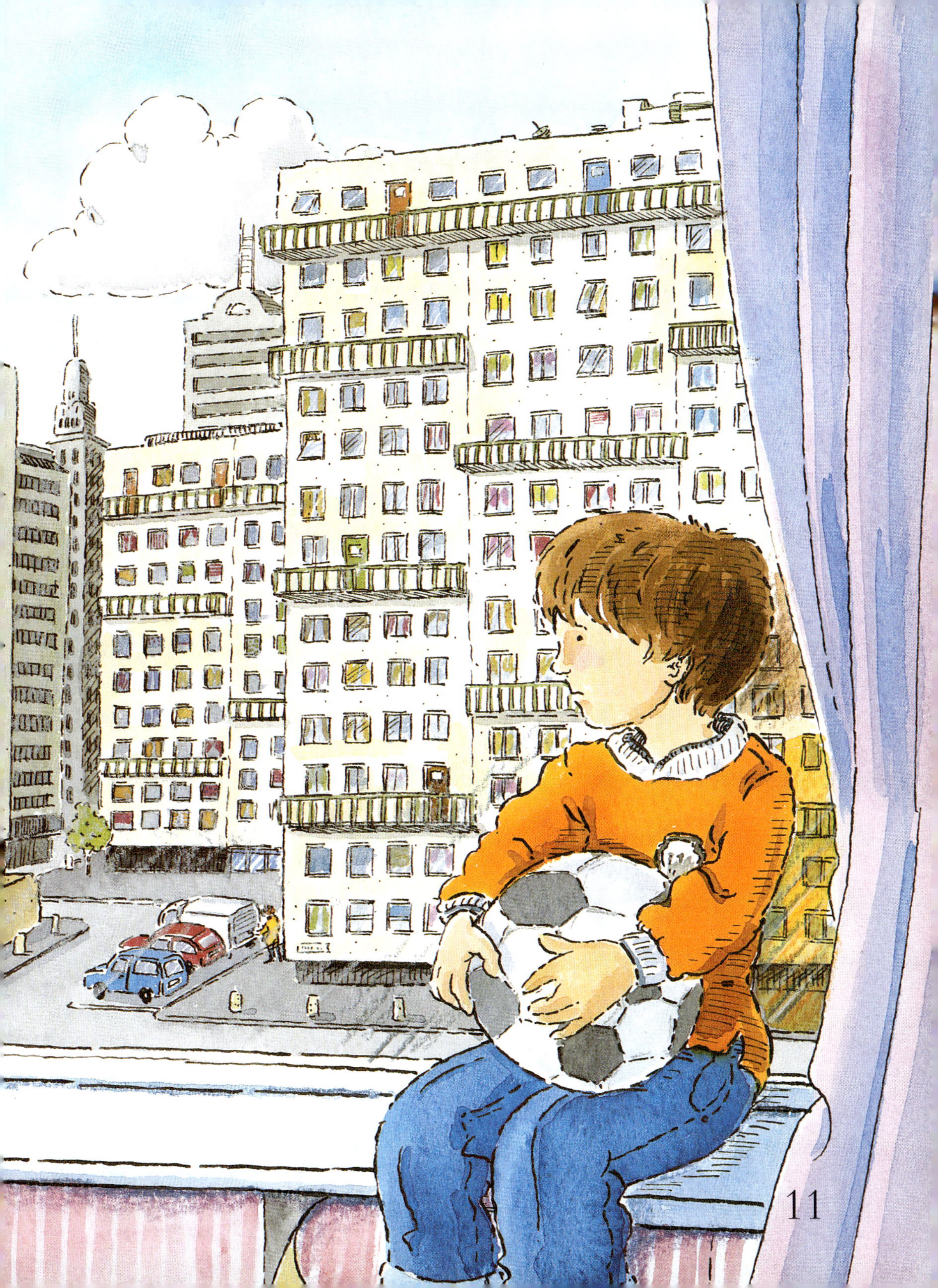

Getting Around

In small towns it doesn't take long to get to school. But if you live in a city, a short journey can take hours! The best thing is to hop on a bus, a tram, or a subway train. Public transportation is important in cities. The fewer cars there are on the roads, the quicker the traffic can move.

13

Under the Streets

In cities, workers are always digging holes in the road. Under the ground, there are pipes and cables to repair. The pipes pump gas and water to every building in the city. The cables carry electricity and telephone lines. We don't see these, but without them the city wouldn't work.

Electricity cables

Gas pipes

Water pipes

Telephone cables

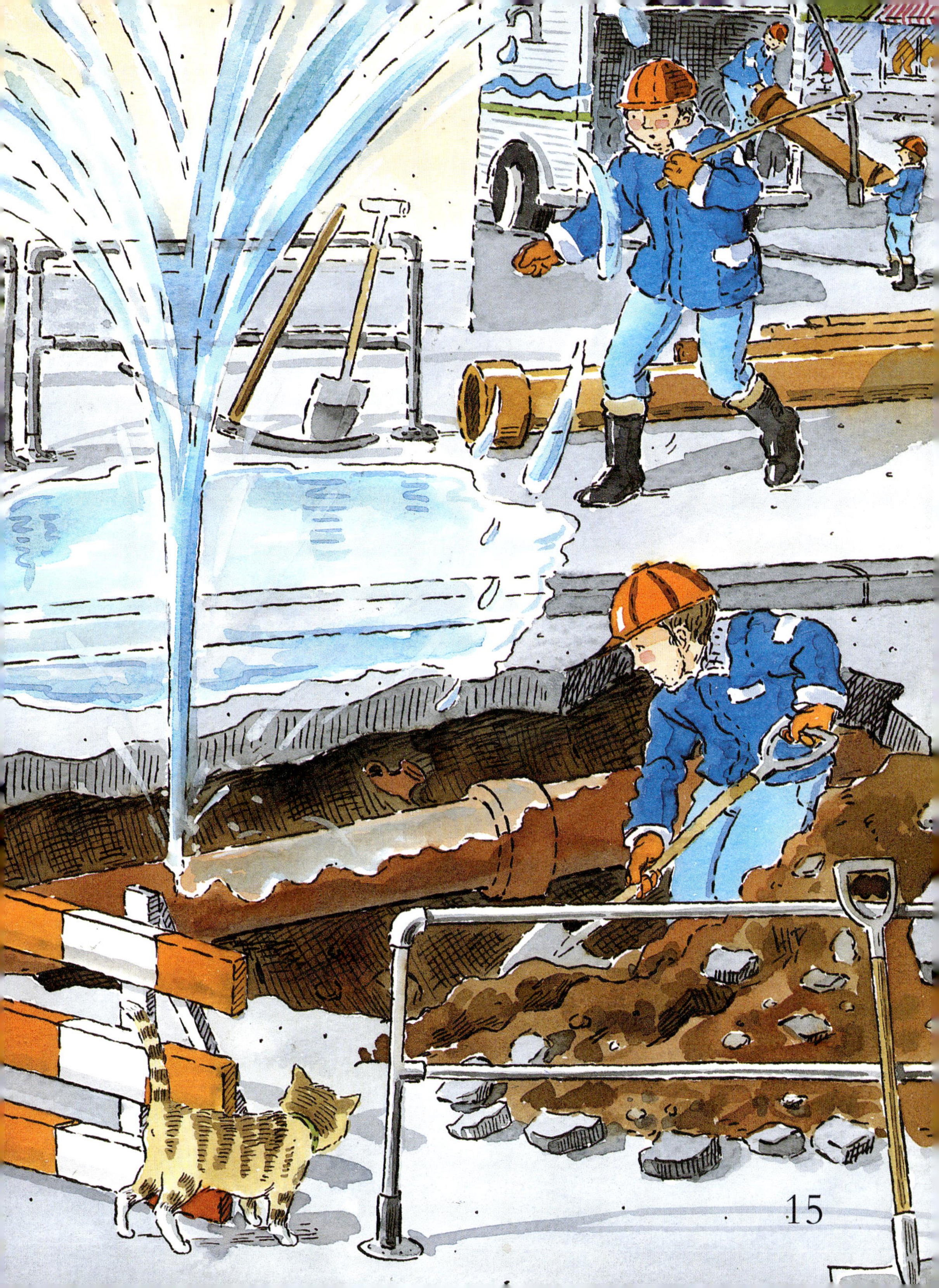

Old and New

Towns are always changing. Old buildings are torn down as new ones are built. Narrow streets make way for wider roads. Some old buildings are protected because they are interesting or beautifully built. An old courthouse, a church, or a tower—many towns have something like this.

17

Fresh Air?

It's hard to keep a city clean. Factory and car fumes poison the air. They damage animals and plants, and make people cough and wheeze. Factories have now moved away from town centers—but we still need to cut down on the cars.

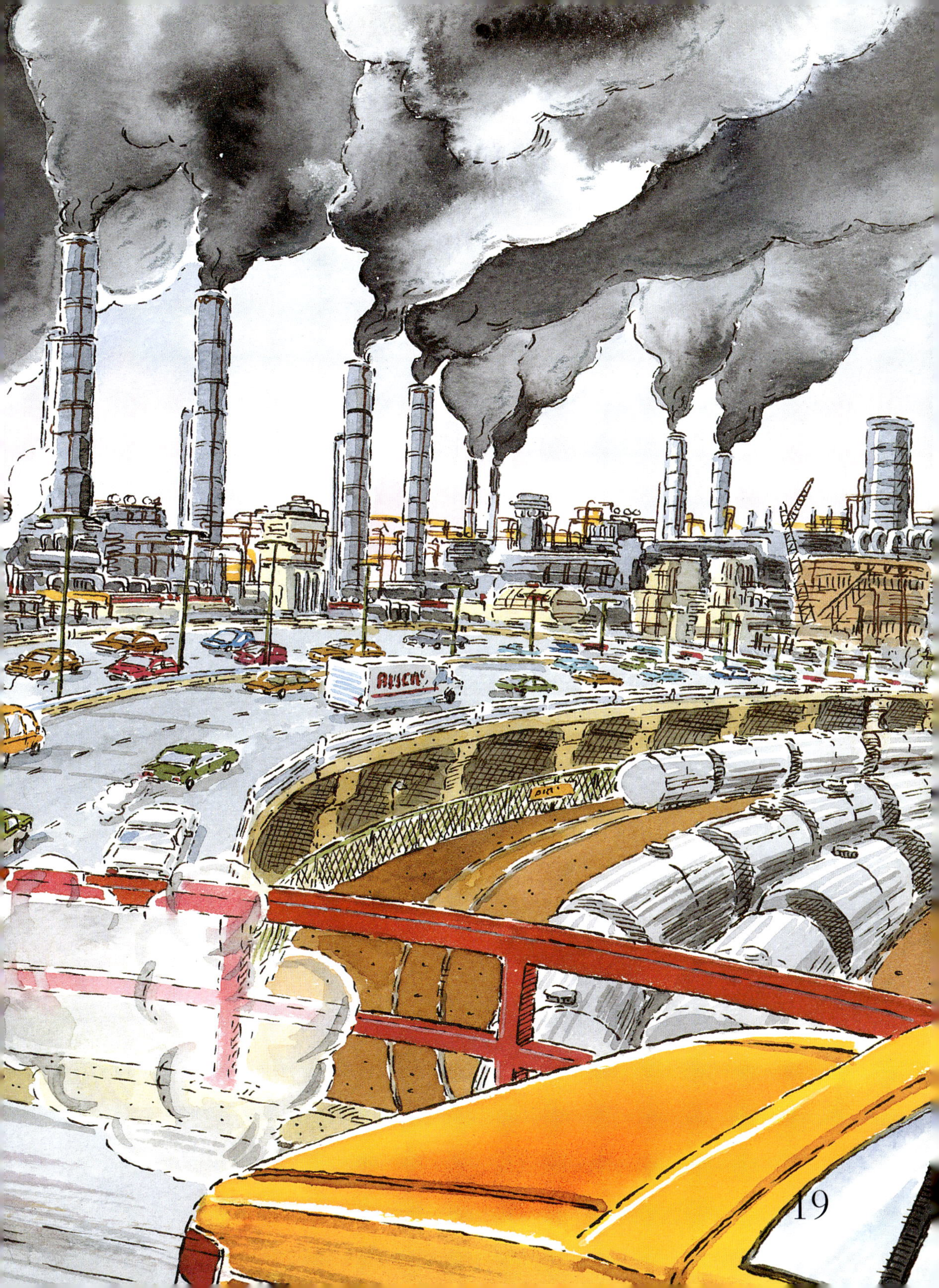

Green in the City

Many towns have parks with tall trees and cool fountains. Away from the busy streets, these are quiet, open spaces where adults can rest and children can play. Cities are hot and sticky in the summer. It's good to sit on the grass or under a shady tree.

21

Free Time

People like to visit cities. If you have some time to spare, you can do anything you want in a city. There are cafés and restaurants, and every kind of store. At weekends, you can go to a museum, a theater, or visit the zoo. During the holiday season there might even be parades or other special events.

Playing tennis

Visiting the zoo